CU00808390

The Vibrant Mediterranean Poultry Recipes Diet Cookbook

Enrich your Poultry Meals with Amazing Recipes

Hanna Briggs

© **Copyright 2020 - All rights reserved.**

The content contained within this book may not be reproduced, duplicated or transmitted without direct written permission from the author or the publisher.

Under no circumstances will any blame or legal responsibility be held against the publisher, or author, for any damages, reparation, or monetary loss due to the information contained within this book. Either directly or indirectly.

Legal Notice:

This book is copyright protected. This book is only for personal use. You cannot amend, distribute, sell, use, quote or paraphrase any part, or the content within this book, without the consent of the author or publisher.

Disclaimer Notice:

Please note the information contained within this document is for educational and entertainment purposes only. All effort has been executed to present accurate, up to date, and reliable, complete information. No warranties of any kind are declared or implied. Readers acknowledge that the author is not engaging in the rendering of legal, financial, medical or professional advice. The content within this book has been derived from various sources. Please consult a licensed professional before attempting any techniques outlined in this book.

By reading this document, the reader agrees that under no circumstances is the author responsible for any losses, direct or indirect, which are incurred as a result of the use of information contained within this document, including, but not limited to, — errors, omissions, or inaccuracies.

Table of contents

Introduction

Consuming the Mediterranean diet minimalizes the use of processed foods. It has been related to a reduced level of risk in developing numerous chronic diseases. It also enhances life expectancy. Several kinds of research have demonstrated many benefits in preventing cardiovascular disease, atrial fibrillation, breast cancer, and type 2 diabetes. Many pieces of evidence indicated a pattern that leads to low lipid, reduction in oxidative stress, platelet aggregation, and inflammation, and modification of growth factors and hormones involved in cancer.

Reduces Heart Diseases

According to research studies, the Mediterranean diet, which focuses on omega-3 ingredients and mono-saturated fats, reduces heart disease risk. It decreases the chances of cardiac death. The use of olive oil maintains the blood pressure levels. It is suitable for reducing hypertension. It also helps in combating the disease-promoting impacts of oxidation. This diet discourages the use of hydrogenated oils and saturated fats, which can cause heart disease.

Weight-loss

If you have been looking for diet plans for losing weight without feeling hungry, the Mediterranean diet can give you long term results. It is one of the best approaches. It is sustainable as it provides the most realistic approach to eat to feel full and energetic. This diet mostly consists of nutrient-dense food. It gives enough room for you to choose between low-carb and lower protein food. Olive oil consumed in this diet has antioxidants, natural vitamins, and some crucial fatty acids. It all improves your overall health. The Mediterranean diet focuses on natural foods, so there is very little room for junk and processed foods contributing to health-related issues and weight gain.

Most people trying the Mediterranean diet have gained positive results in cutting their weight. It is a useful option for someone looking forward to weight-loss as it provides the most unique and simple way to lose the overall calories without even changing your lifestyle that much. When you try to decrease calorie intake, losing weight is inevitable dramatically. But it will not benefit you. It will cause many health problems for you, including severe muscle loss. When you go for a Mediterranean diet, the body moves towards a sustainable model that burns calories slowly. So, it is crucial to practice the right approach and choose fat burning and more effective weight loss.

Prevents Cancer

The cornerstone of this diet is plant-based ingredients, especially vegetables and fruits. They help in preventing cancer. A plant-based diet provides antioxidants that help in protecting your DNA from damage and cell mutation. It also helps in lowering inflammation and delaying tumor growth. Various studies found that olive oil is a natural way to prevent cancer. It also decreases colon and bowel cancers. The plant-based diet balances blood sugar. It also sustains a healthy weight.

Prevents Diabetes

Numerous studies found that this healthy diet functions as an anti-inflammatory pattern, which helps fight the diseases related to chronic inflammation, Type 2 diabetes, and metabolic syndrome. It is considered very effective in preventing diabetes as it controls the insulin levels, which is a hormone to control the blood sugar levels and causes weight gain. Intake of a well-balanced diet consisting of fatty acids alongside some healthy carbohydrates and proteins is the best gift to your body. These foods help your body in burning fats more efficiently, which also provides energy. Due to the consumption of these kinds of foods, the insulin resistance level becomes non-existent, making it impossible to have high blood sugar.

Anti-aging

Choosing a Mediterranean diet without suffering from malnutrition is the most efficient and consistent anti-aging intervention. It undoubtedly expands lifespan, according to the research. The study found that the longevity biomarkers, i.e., body temperature and insulin level, and the DNA damage decreased significantly in humans by the Mediterranean diet. Other mechanisms also prove the claim made by researchers in explaining the anti-aging effects of adopting the Mediterranean diet, including reduced lipid peroxidation, high efficiency of oxidative repair, increased antioxidant defense system, and reduced mitochondrial generation rate.

Maintains Blood Sugar Level

The Mediterranean diet focuses on healthy carbs and whole grains. It has a lot of significant benefits. Consumption of whole-grain foods, like buckwheat, quinoa, and wheat berries instead of refined foods, helps you maintain blood sugar levels that ultimately gives you enough energy for the whole day.

Enhances Cognitive Health

The Mediterranean diet helps in preserving memory. It is one of the most useful steps for Alzheimer's treatment and dementia. Cognitive disorders occur when our brains do not get sufficient dopamine, which is a crucial chemical vital for mood regulation, thought processing, and body movements. Healthy fats like olive oil and nuts are good at fighting cognitive decline, mostly an age-related issue. They help counter some harmful impacts of the free radicals, inflammation, and toxins caused by having a low diet. The Mediterranean diet proves to be beneficial in decreasing

the risk of Alzheimer's to a great extent. Foods like yogurt help in having a healthy gut that improves mood, cognitive functioning, and memory.

Better Endurance Level

Mediterranean diet helps in fat loss and maintains muscle mass. It improves physical performance and enhances endurance levels. Research done on mice has shown positive results in these aspects. It also improves the health of our tissues in the long-term. The growth hormone also offers increased levels as a result of the Mediterranean diet. Which ultimately helps in improving metabolism and body composition.

Keeps You Agile

The nutrients from the Mediterranean diet reduces your risk of muscle weakness and frailty. It increases longevity. When your risk of heart disease reduces, it also reduces the risk of early death. It also strengthens your bones. Certain compounds found in olive oil help in preserving bone density. It helps increase the maturation and proliferation of the bone cells—dietary patterns of the Mediterranean diet help prevent osteoporosis.

Healthy Sleep Patterns

Our eating habits have a considerable impact on sleepiness and wakefulness. Some Mediterranean diet believers have reported an improved sleeping pattern as a result of changing their eating patterns. It has a considerable impact on your sleep because they regulate the circadian rhythm that determines our sleep patterns. If you have a regulated and balanced circadian rhythm, you will fall asleep quite quickly. You will also feel refreshed when you wake up. Another theory states that having the last meal will help you digest the food way before sleep. Digestion works best when you are upright.

Apart from focusing on plant-based eating, the Mediterranean diet philosophy emphasizes variety and moderation, living a life with perfect harmony with nature, valuing relationships in life, including sharing and enjoying meals, and having an entirely active lifestyle. The Mediterranean diet is at the crossroads. With the traditions and culture of three millennia, the Mediterranean diet lifestyle made its way to the medical world a long time ago. It has progressively recognized and became one of the successful and healthiest patterns that lead to a healthy lifestyle.

Besides metabolic, cardiovascular, cognitive, and many other benefits, this diet improves your life quality. Therefore, it is recommended today by many medical professionals worldwide. Efforts are being made in both non--Mediterranean and Mediterranean populations to make everyone benefit from the fantastic network of eating habits and patterns that began in old-time and which became a medical recommendation for a healthy lifestyle.

What to Eat and what to avoid

Fruits and vegetables: Mediterranean diet is one of the plant-based diet plans. Fresh fruits and vegetables contain a large number of vitamins, nutrients, fibers, minerals, and antioxidants

Fruits: Apple, berries, grapes, peaches, fig, grapefruit, dates, melon, oranges and pears.

Vegetables: Spinach, Brussels sprout, kale, tomatoes, kale, summer squash, onion, cauliflower, peppers, cucumbers, turnips, potatoes, sweet potatoes, and parsnips.

Seeds and nuts: Seeds and nuts are rich in monounsaturated fats and omega- 3 fatty acids.

Seeds: pumpkin seeds, flax seeds, sesame seeds, and sunflower seeds. Nuts: Almond, hazelnuts, pistachios, cashews, and walnuts.

Whole grains: Whole grains are high in fibers and they are not processed so they do not contain unhealthy fats like trans-fats compare to processed ones.

Whole grains: Wheat, quinoa, rice, barley, oats, rye, and brown rice. You can also use bread and pasta which is made from whole grains.

Fish and seafood: Fish are the rich source of omega-3 fatty acids and proteins. Eating fish at least once a week is recommended here. The healthiest way to consume fish is to grill it. Grilling fish taste good and never need extra oil.

Fish and seafood: salmon, trout, clams, mackerel, sardines, tuna and shrimp.

Legumes: Legumes (beans) are a rich source of protein, vitamins, and fibers. Regular consumption of beans helps to reduce the risk of diabetes, cancer and heart disease.

Legumes: Kidney beans, peas, chickpeas, black beans, fava beans, lentils, and pinto beans.

Spices and herbs: Spices and herbs are used to add the taste to your meal.

Spices and herbs: mint, thyme, garlic, basil, cinnamon, nutmeg, rosemary, oregano and more.

Healthy fats: Olive oil is the main fat used in the Mediterranean diet. It helps to reduce the risk of inflammatory disorder, diabetes, cancer, and heart- related disease. It also helps to increase HDL (good cholesterol) levels and decrease LDL (bad cholesterol) levels into your body. It also helps to lose weight.

Fats: Olive oil, avocado oil, walnut oil, extra virgin olive oil, avocado, and olives.

Dairy: Moderate amounts of dairy products are allowed during the Mediterranean diet. The dairy product contains high amounts of fats.

Dairy: Greek yogurt, skim milk and cheese.

Food to avoid

Refined grains: Refined grains are not allowed in a Mediterranean diet. It raises your blood sugar level. Refined grains like white bread, white rice, and pasta.

Refined oils: Oils like vegetable oils, cottonseed oils, and soybean oils are completely avoided from the Mediterranean diet. It raises your LDL (bad cholesterol) level.

Added Sugar: Added sugar is not allowed in the Mediterranean diet. These types of artificial sugars are found in table sugar, soda, chocolate, ice cream, and candies. It raises your blood sugar level.

You should consume only natural sugars in the Mediterranean diet.

Processed foods: Generally Processed foods come in boxes. Its low-fat food should not be eaten during the diet. It contains a high amount of trans-fats. Mediterranean diet is all about to eat fresh and natural food.

Trans-fat and saturated fats: In this category of food contains butter and margarine.

Processed Meat: Mediterranean diet does not allow to use of processed meat such as bacon, hot dogs and sausage.

Poultry Recipes

Chicken Shawarma
Servings: 8

Ingredients:

- 2 lb. chicken breast, sliced into strips
- 1 teaspoon paprika
- teaspoon ground cumin
- 1/4 teaspoon granulated garlic
- 1/2 teaspoon turmeric
- 1/4 teaspoon ground allspice

Directions:

1.   Season the chicken with the spices, and a little salt and pepper.

2.   Pour 1 cup chicken broth to the skillet.

3.   Seal the skillet.

4.   Choose poultry setting.

5.   Cook for 15 minutes.

6.   Release the pressure naturally.

Honey Balsamic Chicken
Servings: 10

Ingredients:

- 1/4 cup honey
- 1/2 cup balsamic vinegar
- 1/4 cup soy sauce
- 2   cloves garlic minced
- 10 chicken drumsticks

Directions:

1. Mix the honey, vinegar, soy sauce and garlic in a bowl.

2. Marinate the chicken in the sauce for 30 minutes.

3. Cover the skillet.

4. Set it to manual.

5. Cook at high pressure for 10 minutes.

6. Release the pressure quickly.

7. Choose the saute button to thicken the sauce

Garlic And Lemon Chicken Dish
Servings: 4

Ingredients

- 2-3 pounds chicken breast
- 1 teaspoon salt
- 1 onion, diced
- 1 tablespoon ghee
- 5 garlic cloves, minced
- ½ cup organic chicken broth 1 teaspoon dried parsley

- 1 large lemon, juiced
- 3-4   teaspoon arrowroot flour

Directions

1.   Set your skillet to Saute mode. Add diced up onion and cooking fat

2.   Allow the onions to cook for 5 -10 minutes

3.   Add the rest of the ingredients except arrowroot flour

4.   Lock up the lid and set the skillet to poultry mode. Cook until the timer runs out

5.   Allow the pressure to release naturally

6.   Once done, remove ¼ cup of the sauce from the skillet and add arrowroot to make a slurry

7.   Add the slurry to the skillet to make the gravy thick. Keep stirring well. Serve!

High-Quality Belizean Chicken Stew

Servings: 4

Ingredients

- 4 whole chicken
- tablespoon coconut oil
- tablespoons achiote seasoning
- 2 tablespoons white vinegar
- tablespoons Worcestershire sauce
- 1 cup yellow onion, sliced
- garlic cloves, sliced
- teaspoon ground cumin
- 1 teaspoon dried oregano
- ½ teaspoon black pepper
- 2 cups chicken stock

Directions

1.   Take a large sized bowl and add achiote paste, vinegar, Worcestershire sauce, oregano, cumin and pepper. Mix well and add chicken pieces and rub the marinade all over them

2.   Allow the chicken to sit overnight. Set your skillet to Saute mode and add coconut oil

3.   Once the oil is hot, add the chicken pieces to the skillet and brown them in batches (each batch for 2 minutes). Remove the seared chicken and transfer them to a plate

4.   Add onions, garlic to the skillet and Saute for 2-3 minutes . Add chicken pieces back to the skillet

5.   Pour chicken broth to the bowl with marinade and stir well. Add the mixture to the skillet

6.   Seal up the lid and cook for about 20 minutes at high pressure

7.   Once done, release the pressure naturally . Season with a bit of salt and serve!

Crispy Mediterranean Chicken Thighs
Servings: 6

Ingredients

- 2   tablespoons extra-virgin olive oil
- 2 teaspoons dried rosemary
- 1½ teaspoons ground cumin
- 1½ teaspoons ground coriander
- ¾ teaspoon dried oregano
- ⅛ teaspoon salt
- 6 bone-in, skin-on chicken thighs (about 3 pounds)

Directions

1.   Preheat the oven to 450°F. Line a baking sheet with parchment paper.

2.   Place the olive oil and spices into a large bowl and mix together, making a paste. Add the chicken and mix together until evenly coated. Place on the prepared baking sheet.

3.   Bake for 30 to 35 minutes, or until golden brown and the chicken registers an internal temperature of 165°F.

Greek Penne and Chicken
Servings: 4

Ingredients

- 16-ounce package of Penne Pasta
- pound of Skinless Boneless Chicken Breast Halves (Cut Into Bite Sized Pieces)
- 1/2 cup of Chopped Red Onion
- 1 1/2 tablespoons of Butter

- cloves of Minced Garlic
- 14-ounce can of Artichoke Hearts
- 1 Chopped Tomato
- tablespoons of Chopped Fresh Parsley
- 1/2 cup of Crumbled Feta Cheese
- 2 tablespoons of Lemon Juice
- 1 teaspoon of Dried Oregano Ground Black Pepper
- Salt

Directions

1.   In a large sized skillet over a medium-high heat, melt your butter. Add your garlic and onion. Cook approximately 2 minutes. Add your chopped chicken and continue to cook until golden brown. Should take approximately 5 to 6 minutes. Stir occasionally.

2.   Reduce your heat to a medium-low. Drain and chop your artichoke hearts. Add them to your skillet along with your chopped tomato, fresh parsley, feta cheese, dried oregano, lemon juice, and drained pasta. Cook for 2 to 3 minutes until heated through.

3.   Season with your ground black pepper and salt.

4.   Serve and Enjoy!

Yogurt-Marinated Chicken Kebabs
Servings: 4

Ingredients:

- ½ cup plain Greek yogurt
- 1 tablespoon lemon juice
- ½ teaspoon ground cumin
- ½ teaspoon ground coriander
- ½ teaspoon kosher salt
- ¼ teaspoon cayenne pepper
- 1½ pound skinless, boneless chicken breast, cut into 1-inch cubes

Directions

1.   In a large bowl or zip-top bag, combine the yogurt, lemon juice, cumin, coriander, salt, and cayenne pepper. Mix together thoroughly and then add the chicken. Marinate for at least 30 minutes, and up to overnight in the refrigerator.

2. Bake for 20 minutes, turning the chicken over once halfway through the cooking time.

Braised Chicken with Roasted Bell Peppers
Servings: 8

Ingredients:

- 2 tablespoons extra-virgin olive oil
- 4 pounds bone-in chicken, breast and thighs, skin removed
- 1½ teaspoon kosher salt, divided
- ¼ teaspoon freshly ground black pepper
- 1 onion, julienned
- 6 garlic cloves, sliced
- cup white wine
- pounds tomatoes, chopped
- ¼ teaspoon red pepper flakes

- bell peppers (any colors you like) or 2 jars roasted red peppers, drained
- ⅓ cup fresh parsley, chopped 1 tablespoon lemon juice

Directions

1.   Heat the olive oil in a large Dutch oven or skillet over medium- high heat. Season the chicken with ¾ teaspoon of the salt and the pepper. Add half the chicken to the skillet and brown about 2 minutes on each side. Transfer to a plate, and repeat with the remaining half of the chicken.

2.   Lower the heat to medium and add the onion. Sauté for about 5 minutes. Add the garlic and sauté for 30 seconds. Add the wine, increase the heat to medium-high, and bring to a boil to deglaze the skillet, scraping up any brown bits on the bottom. Reduce the liquid by half, about 5 to 7 minutes. Add the tomatoes, red pepper flakes, and the remaining ¾ teaspoon salt and mix well. Add the chicken back to the skillet, cover, reduce the heat to low, and simmer for 40 minutes, turning the chicken halfway through the cooking time.

3.   While the chicken cooks, prepare the roasted bell peppers. If you are using raw peppers, please refer to the roasting method here. If using jarred roasted red peppers, move on to step 4.

4.   Chop the bell peppers into 1-inch pieces and set aside.

5.   Once the chicken is cooked through, transfer it to a plate.

6.   Increase the heat to high and bring the mixture to a boil. Reduce by half, about 10 minutes.

7.   When the chicken is cool enough to handle, remove the meat from the bone and return it to the skillet with the bell peppers. Simmer 5 minutes to heat through. Stir in the parsley and lemon juice.

Chicken Stew with Artichokes, Capers, and Olives
Servings: 4

Ingredients:

- 1½ pounds boneless, skinless chicken thighs 1 teaspoon kosher salt, divided
- ¼ teaspoon freshly ground black pepper
- 2 tablespoons olive oil
- 1 onion, julienned
- 4 garlic cloves, sliced

- 1 teaspoon ground turmeric
- 1 teaspoon ground cumin
- ½ teaspoon ground coriander
- ½ teaspoon ground cinnamon
- ¼ teaspoon red pepper flakes
- 1 dried bay leaf
- 1¼ cups no-salt-added chicken stock
- ¼ cup white wine vinegar
- 2 tablespoons lemon juice 1 tablespoon lemon zest
- 1 (14-ounce) can artichoke hearts, drained
- ¼ cup olives, pitted and chopped
- 1 teaspoon capers, rinsed and chopped
- 1 tablespoon fresh mint, chopped
- 1 tablespoon fresh parsley, chopped

Directions

1.   Season the chicken with ½ teaspoon of salt and pepper.

2.   Heat the olive oil in a large skillet or sauté pan over medium heat. Add the chicken and sauté 2 to 3 minutes per side. Transfer to a plate and set aside.

3.   Add the onion to the same pan and sauté until translucent, about

5 minutes. Add the garlic and sauté 30 seconds. Add the remaining ½ teaspoon salt, the turmeric, cumin, coriander, cinnamon, red pepper flakes, and bay leaf and sauté 30 seconds.

4.   Add ¼ cup of the chicken stock and increase the heat to medium-high to deglaze the pan, scraping up any brown bits on the bottom. Add the remaining 1 cup stock, the lemon juice, and lemon zest. Cover, lower the heat to low, and simmer for 10 minutes.

5.   Add the artichokes, olives, and capers and mix well. Add the reserved chicken and nestle it into the mixture. Simmer, uncovered, until the chicken fully cooks through, about 10 to 15 minutes. Garnish with the mint and parsley.

Za'atar Chicken Tenders
Servings: 4

Ingredients:

- Olive oil cooking spray
- 1 pound chicken tenders
- 1½ tablespoons za'atar
- ½ teaspoon kosher salt
- ¼ teaspoon freshly ground black pepper

Directions

1.   In a large bowl, combine the chicken, za'atar, salt, and black pepper.

2.   Mix together well, covering the chicken tenders fully.

3.   Arrange in a single layer on the baking sheet and bake for 15 minutes, turning the chicken over once halfway through the cooking time.

Lemon Chicken with Artichokes and Crispy Kale
Servings: 4

Ingredients:

- 3 tablespoons extra-virgin olive oil, divided
- 2 tablespoons lemon juice
- Zest of 1 lemon
- 2 garlic cloves, minced
- 2 teaspoons dried rosemary
- ¼ teaspoon freshly ground black pepper
- 1½ pounds boneless, skinless chicken breast
- 2 (14-ounce) cans artichoke hearts, drained
- 1 bunch (about 6 ounces) lacinato kale, stemmed and torn or chopped into pieces

Directions

1.   In a large bowl or zip-top bag, combine 2 tablespoons of the olive oil, the lemon juice, lemon zest, garlic, rosemary, salt, and black pepper. Mix well and then add the chicken and artichokes. Marinate for at least 30 minutes, and up to 4 hours in the refrigerator.

2.   Remove the chicken and artichokes from the marinade and spread them in a single layer on the baking sheet. Roast for 15 minutes, turn the chicken over, and roast another 15 minutes. Remove the baking sheet and put the chicken, artichokes, and juices on a platter or large plate. Tent with foil to keep warm.

3.   Change the oven temperature to broil. In a large bowl, combine the kale with the remaining 1 tablespoon of the olive oil.

Arrange the kale on the baking sheet and broil until golden brown in sskillets and as crispy as you like, about 3 to 5 minutes.

4.   Place the kale on top of the chicken and artichokes.

Sumac Chicken with Cauliflower and Carrots
Servings: 4

Ingredients:

- 3 tablespoons extra-virgin olive oil
- 1 tablespoon ground sumac
- teaspoon kosher salt
- ½ teaspoon ground cumin
- ¼ teaspoon freshly ground black pepper
- 1½ pounds bone-in chicken thighs and drumsticks
- 1 medium cauliflower, cut into 1-inch florets
- carrots, peeled and cut into 1-inch rounds
- 1 lemon, cut into ¼-inch-thick slices
- 1 tablespoon lemon juice

- ¼ cup fresh parsley, chopped
- ¼ cup fresh mint, chopped

Directions

1.   Preheat the oven to 425°F. Line a baking sheet with parchment paper or foil.

2.   In a large bowl, whisk together the olive oil, sumac, salt, cumin, and black pepper. Add the chicken, cauliflower, and carrots and toss until thoroughly coated with the oil and spice mixture.

3.   Arrange the cauliflower, carrots, and chicken in a single layer on the baking sheet. Top with the lemon slices. Roast for 40 minutes, tossing the vegetables once halfway through. Sprinkle the lemon juice over the chicken and vegetables and garnish with the parsley and mint.

Harissa Yogurt Chicken Thighs
Servings: 4

Ingredients:

- ½ cup plain Greek yogurt
- 2 tablespoons harissa
- tablespoon lemon juice
- ¼ teaspoon freshly ground black pepper
- 1½ pounds boneless, skinless chicken thighs

Directions

1. In a bowl, combine the yogurt, harissa, lemon juice, salt, and black pepper. Add the chicken and mix together. Marinate for at least 15 minutes, and up to 4 hours in the refrigerator.

2.   Remove the chicken thighs from the marinade and arrange in a single layer on the baking sheet. Roast for 20 minutes, turning the chicken over halfway.

3.   Change the oven temperature to broil. Broil the chicken until golden brown in skillets, 2 to 3 minutes.

Braised Chicken with Wild Mushrooms
Servings: 4

Ingredients

- 1/4 cup dried porcini or morel mushrooms
- 1/4 cup olive oil
- 2–3 slices low-salt turkey bacon, chopped
- 1 chicken, cut into pieces
- Sea salt and freshly ground pepper, to taste
- 1 small celery stalk, diced
- 1 small dried red chili, chopped
- 1/4 cup vermouth or white wine

- 1/4 cup tomato puree
- 1/4 cup low-salt chicken stock
- 1/2 teaspoon arrowroot
- 1/4 cup flat-leaf parsley, chopped
- 4 teaspoons fresh thyme, chopped
- 3 teaspoons fresh tarragon

Directions

1. Place the mushrooms in a small bowl and pour boiling water over them. Allow them to stand for 20 minutes to soften.

2. Drain and chop, reserving the liquid.

3. Heat the olive oil on medium heat. Add the bacon and cook until browned and slightly crisp. Drain the bacon on a paper towel.

4. Season the chicken with sea salt and freshly ground pepper, and add to the oil and bacon drippings.

5. Cook for 10–15 minutes, turning halfway through the cooking time so that both sides of the chicken are golden brown.

6. Add the celery and the chopped chili, and cook for 3–5 minutes or until soft.

7. Deglaze the pan with the wine, using a wooden spoon to scrape up the brown bits stuck to the bottom.

8. Add the tomato puree, chicken stock, arrowroot, and mushroom liquid. Cover and simmer on low for 45 minutes.

9. Add the fresh chopped herbs and cook an additional 10 minutes, until the sauce thickens.

10. Season with freshly ground pepper and sea salt to taste. Serve with wilted greens or crunchy green beans.

Braised Duck with Fennel Root
Servings: 6

Ingredients

- 1/4 cup olive oil
- 1 whole duck, cleaned
- 3 teaspoon fresh rosemary
- 2 garlic cloves, minced
- Sea salt and freshly ground pepper, to taste
- 3 fennel bulbs, cut into chunks
- 1/2 cup sherry

Directions

1. Preheat the oven to 375 degrees.

2. Heat the olive oil in a Dutch oven.

3. Season the duck, including the cavity, with the rosemary, garlic, sea salt, and freshly ground pepper.

4. Place the duck in the oil, and cook it for 10–15 minutes, turning as necessary to brown all sides.

5.   Add the fennel bulbs and cook an additional 5 minutes.

6.   Pour the sherry over the duck and fennel, cover and cook in the oven for 30–45 minutes, or until internal temperature of the duck is 140–150 degrees at its thickest part.

7.   Allow duck to sit for 15 minutes before serving.

Chicken Tagine with Olives
Servings: 6

Ingredients

- 1 teaspoon ground ginger
- 1/2 teaspoon ground cumin
- 1/2 teaspoon paprika
- Sea salt and freshly ground peppe
- 1/2 teaspoon turmeric
- Pinch saffron threads
- 1 clove garlic, minced
- 1 whole chicken
- 2 medium onions, thinly sliced
- 1/2 cup finely chopped flatleaf parsley
- 1/2 cup finely chopped cilantro
- 1 cinnamon stick
- 3 cups water
- 2 tablespoons olive oil

- 1 tablespoon butter
- zest and Juice of 1 lemon
- 1 cup green or purple olives

Directions

1.	Combine the spices and garlic in a small bowl.

2.	Pat the chicken dry, brush the spices over the chicken, and massage them in with your fingers, including in the cavity.

3.	Place the chicken in a Dutch oven.

4.	Add the onions, parsley, cilantro, and cinnamon along with the water.

5.	Bring the water to a boil and add the olive oil, butter, and lemon zest and juice.

6.	Cover and simmer for 1–2 hours, or until the chicken is tender and the sauce has reduced and thickened slightly.

7.	Remove the lid and simmer an additional 15 minutes. Season with freshly ground pepper and sea salt to taste.

8.	Add the olives immediately before serving.

Citrus Chicken with Pecan Wild Rice
Servings: 4

Ingredients

- 4 boneless, skinless chicken breasts
- Sea salt and freshly ground pepper, to taste
- 2 tablespoons olive oil
- Juice and zest of 1 orange
- 2 cups wild rice, cooked
- 2 green onions, sliced
- 1 cup pecans, toasted and chopped

Directions

1.   Season chicken breasts with sea salt and freshly ground pepper.

2.   Heat a large skillet over medium heat. Add the oil and sear the chicken until browned on 1 side.

3.   Flip the chicken and brown other side.

4.   Add the orange juice to the skillet and let cook down.

5.   In a large bowl, combine the rice, onions, pecans, and orange zest. Season with freshly ground pepper and sea salt to taste.

6.   Serve the chicken alongside the rice and a green salad for a complete meal.

Marinated Chicken

Servings: 4

Ingredients

- 1/2 cup olive oil
- 2 tablespoon fresh rosemary
- 1 teaspoon minced garlic
- Juice and zest of 1 lemon
- 1/4 cup chopped flat-leaf parsley
- Sea salt and freshly ground pepper, to taste
- 4 boneless, skinless chicken breasts

Directions

1. Mix all ingredients except the chicken together in a plastic bag or bowl.

2. Place the chicken in the container and shake/stir so the marinade thoroughly coats the chicken.

3. Refrigerate up to 24 hours.

4. Heat a grill to medium heat and cook the chicken for 6–8 minutes a side. Turn only once during the cooking process.

5. Serve with a Greek salad and brown rice.

Niçoise Chicken
Servings: 6

Ingredients

- 1/4 cup olive oil
- 3 medium onions, coarsely chopped
- 3 cloves garlic, minced
- 4 pounds chicken breast from 1 cut-up chicken
- 5 Roma tomatoes, peeled and chopped
- 1/2 cup white wine
- • 1 (14-1/2 ounce) can chicken broth
- 1/2 cup black Niçoise olives, pitted
- Juice of 1 lemon
- 1/4 cup flat-leaf parsley, chopped

- 1 tablespoon fresh tarragon leaves, chopped
- • Sea salt and freshly ground pepper, to taste

Directions

1.   Heat the olive oil in a deep saucepan over medium heat. Cook the onions and garlic 5 minutes, or until tender and translucent.

2.   Add the chicken and cook an additional 5 minutes to brown slightly.

3.   Add the tomatoes, white wine, and chicken broth, cover, and simmer 30–45 minutes on medium-low heat, or until the chicken is tender and the sauce is thickened slightly.

4.   Remove the lid and add the olives and lemon juice.

5.   Cook an additional 10–15 minutes to thicken the sauce further.

6.   Stir in the parsley and tarragon, and season to taste. Serve immediately with noodles or potatoes and a dark leafy salad.

Turkish Chicken Kebabs
Servings: 6

Ingredients

- 2 white onions, chopped

- 2 garlic cloves, crushed

- ¾ cup extra-virgin olive oil, divided

- 2 tablespoons lemon juice

- 1 teaspoon dried oregano

- 2 teaspoons salt, divided

- ½ teaspoon curry powder

- ½ teaspoon ground turmeric

- 1 ½ pounds boneless chicken breast or thigh meat, cut into 1-inch pieces

- 12 skewers

- 2 red onions, cut into 1-inch pieces

- 3 to 4 zucchini, cut into 1-inch rounds

- ¼ teaspoon freshly ground black pepper

- ½ lemon

- 1 tablespoon chopped fresh mint

Directions

1. Place the onions, garlic, ½ cup olive oil, lemon juice, oregano, 1 teaspoon salt, curry powder, and turmeric in a blender or food processor and process until puréed.

2. Place the chicken in a medium bowl, pour the marinade over, cover, and marinate in the refrigerator for at least 30 minutes, or overnight.

3. Thread the skewers by beginning with a piece of red onion, a piece of chicken, a piece of zucchini, a piece of chicken, and another piece of red onion. Place the skewers on a baking sheet.

4. When all the skewers have been made, brush with the remaining ¼ cup olive oil and sprinkle with 1 teaspoon salt and the pepper.

5. Heat a grill or broiler until hot. Cook the skewers over a hot grill or in a broiler until the meat is cooked, about 6 to 8 minutes per side.

6. Season the cooked kebabs with freshly squeezed lemon juice and garnish with chopped mint.

7. Let the kebabs sit for about 5 minutes before serving.

8. After the meat has marinated, the skewers can be made and kept in the refrigerator for several hours before grilling. Once cooked, the chicken can be stored in the refrigerator for about 1 week.

Chicken Fra Diavolo
Servings: 6

Ingredients

- 8 chicken thighs, skin on and bone

- 1 teaspoon salt

- ¼ teaspoon freshly ground black pepper

- ¼ cup extra-virgin olive oil

- 1 large onion, sliced

- 3 garlic cloves, minced

- 1 teaspoon red pepper flakes (or to taste)

- 1 teaspoon smoked paprika

- 1 cup red wine

- 1 (14.5-ounce) can fire-roasted tomatoes

- 1 teaspoon dried oregano

- 2 tablespoons chopped fresh flatleaf parsley

Directions

1. Sprinkle the chicken with the salt and pepper.

2. Place a Dutch oven with a lid over high heat. Add the olive oil and brown the chicken on all sides, about 3 to 4 minutes a side. Remove the chicken and set aside.

3. Place the onion, garlic, red pepper flakes, and paprika and cook about 3 minutes to soften the onion. Add the wine, tomatoes, and oregano and bring to a boil.

4. Reduce to a simmer and return the chicken to the skillet. Cover and simmer about 40 minutes or until the chicken is firm.

5. Arrange on a serving platter, garnish with parsley, and serve.

6. The sauce can be made ahead, without the chicken, and stored in the freezer. The entire dish can be stored for 1 week in the refrigerator or for several months in the freezer. Since the recipe makes a fairly large quantity, it's best to freeze it in single or double portions.

Chicken Almond Phyllo Pie
Servings: 8

Ingredients

- 2 tablespoons butter

- 2 tablespoons extra-virgin olive oil

- 1 large onion, chopped

- 2 garlic cloves, chopped

- 1¾ teaspoons ground cinnamon, divided

- 1 teaspoon cayenne pepper

- 1 teaspoon powdered ginger

- ½ teaspoon ground turmeric

- ¼ cup chicken broth or water

- 1 pound boneless chicken thigh meat, chopped into ¼-inch pieces

- 1 teaspoon salt

- ¼ teaspoon freshly ground black pepper

- ¼ cup finely chopped Preserved Lemons or 2 tablespoons lemon juice

- ¼ cup chopped fresh flatleaf parsley

- 4 eggs, beaten

- 1 cup ground unsalted almonds

- 2 tablespoons sugar

- 6 ounces butter, melted

- 12 sheets phyllo (filo)

- ⅓ cup powdered sugar

Directions

1. Place a Dutch oven with a lid over high heat and add the butter and olive oil.

2. Add the onion and garlic and sauté several minutes. Add 1 teaspoon cinnamon, the cayenne, ginger, and turmeric and sauté 5 minutes.

3. To the skillet, add the broth, chicken, salt, and pepper, and simmer 10 minutes or until the chicken is cooked through and the liquid has evaporated. Remove the chicken from the skillet and place in a large bowl. Let cool at least 15 minutes.

4. Add the preserved lemons or lemon juice, parsley, and eggs. Set aside.

5.   In a small bowl, combine the ground almonds, sugar, and ½ teaspoon cinnamon and set aside.

6.   Preheat the oven to 375°F.

7.   Brush a 9-by-13-inch baking pan with a little melted butter.

8.   Place 1 sheet of phyllo in the buttered pan and brush with more butter. Top with another layer of phyllo and brush with butter, then add a third layer and brush with butter.

9.   Sprinkle one-half of the almond mixture over the phyllo. Top with three more sheets of phyllo, brushing each sheet with butter. Spoon one-half of the chicken over the phyllo. Top with three sheets of phyllo, brushing in between each sheet with butter. Add the remaining almond mixture. Finish the dish with the remaining chicken followed by the last three sheets of phyllo, brushing with butter in between each sheet.

10.   Brush the top layer with butter. Using a sharp knife, score the top layers of phyllo into 12 pieces. This will prevent the phyllo from cracking as it rises in the oven.

11.   Bake for 25 to 35 minutes or until golden brown. Remove from the oven and let cool for 10 minutes. Sprinkle with powdered sugar and the remaining ¼ teaspoon cinnamon. Serve warm.

Oven-Poached Chicken with Tarragon
Servings: 4

Ingredients

- 6 boneless, skinless chicken breasts

- ½ cup white wine

- 1 cup chicken broth or water

- 1 shallot, sliced

- 3 sprigs fresh tarragon, plus 1 teaspoon chopped for garnish

- 1 teaspoon salt

- ¼ teaspoon freshly ground black pepper

Directions

1.   Preheat the oven to 375°F.

2.   Place the chicken breasts in a single layer in a 9-by-13-inch pan.

3.   Add the wine, broth or water, shallot, tarragon sprigs, salt, and pepper. Gently stir to combine ingredients.

4.   Cover with foil and place in the oven for 25 to 35 minutes, or until the chicken is firm to the touch.

5.   Carefully remove the foil, since it will release hot steam. Let the chicken rest 10 minutes in the poaching liquid before serving.

6.   Remove the chicken from the pan with a slotted spoon and garnish with the chopped tarragon.

7.   Poached chicken can be stored in the refrigerator for 1 week.

Chicken Breast Stuffed with Sun-Dried Tomatoes and Ricotta

Servings: 4

Ingredients

- 4 ounces ricotta cheese

- 2 tablespoons chopped sun-dried tomatoes

- 1 garlic clove, chopped

- ½ teaspoon chopped fresh thyme

- 1½ teaspoons salt, divided

- 4 boneless, skin-on chicken breasts

- 2 tablespoons extra-virgin olive oil

- ¼ teaspoon freshly ground black pepper

- 1 cup white wine

- ½ lemon

Directions

1. Preheat the oven to 375°F.

2. In a small bowl, combine the ricotta, sun-dried tomatoes, garlic, thyme, and ½ teaspoon salt.

3. Place the chicken skin side up on a work surface.

4. Slide your fingers under the skin and gently pull the skin partially away from the chicken breast, being careful not to tear it.

5. Place about 2 tablespoons of filling under the skin of each breast.

6. Place the stuffed breasts, skin side up, in a 9-inch-square baking dish, tucking the ends of the breasts under so that the breasts are plump and round.

7. Brush the breasts with olive oil and sprinkle with the remaining 1 teaspoon salt and the pepper.

8. Pour the wine into the pan, and bake 35 to 45 minutes or until the skin is golden brown.

9. Remove from the oven and squeeze the lemon juice over the stuffed breasts.

10. Let rest 10 minutes before serving.

11. The breasts can be stored in the refrigerator for 5 days.

Chicken Roasted with 40 Cloves of Garlic
Servings: 4

Ingredients

- 1 whole chicken

- 1 teaspoon salt

- ¼ teaspoon freshly ground black pepper

- 2 tablespoons butter

- 2 tablespoons extra-virgin olive oil

- 40 garlic cloves (about 3 to 4 heads), peeled

- 1 cup white wine

- 1 sprig fresh thyme

Directions

1. Preheat the oven to 375°F.

2. Pat the chicken dry with a paper towel and sprinkle with the salt and pepper.

3. Place a large Dutch oven with a lid over high heat. Add the butter and olive oil. Brown the chicken on all sides, about 5 to 7 minutes per side, using tongs to carefully turn it without breaking the skin.

4. Remove the chicken and set aside.

5. Add the garlic to the same skillet and sauté for 5 minutes to soften. Return the chicken to the skillet and add the wine and thyme.

6. Cover the skillet and place it in the oven for 1 hour.

7. Carefully remove the chicken from the skillet and let it rest for 15 minutes.

8. Carve the chicken and arrange it on a platter. Remove the thyme sprig. Spoon the garlic and pan drippings over the chicken and serve.

Roman Chicken with Peppers
Servings: 4

Ingredients

- 2 tbsp. virgin olive oil
- 8 skinless, boneless chicken thighs
- Kosher salt and freshly ground black pepper
- 1 yellow bell pepper, cut into 1/2 inch slices
- 2 garlic cloves, minced
- 1 tbsp. chopped thyme

- 1 tbsp. chopped oregano

- 1 cup dry white wine

- 1 can (15 oz.) diced tomatoes

- 1/2 cup chicken broth

- 2 tbsp. capers

- 1/2 cup chopped parsley

Directions

1. In a large skillet over medium-high heat add the oil and heat until shimmering.

2. Season chicken with salt and pepper.

3. Working in batches, cook the thighs, turning once, 6 minutes or until browned all over.

4. Transfer to a plate and repeat with remaining thighs, adding more oil as necessary.

5. Reduce heat to medium. Add the peppers and cook, stirring often, 5 minutes or until tender Add the garlic and cook, stirring, 1 minute or until fragrant.

6. Stir in the thyme, oregano and wine; cook, scraping up any browned bits from the bottom of the skillet, 5 minutes.

7. Stir in the tomatoes and broth. Return the chicken to the skillet.

8. Cover and cook, 15 to 20 minutes or until an instant-read thermometer inserted into the thickest part of the thigh registers 165°F and the juices run clear when pierced with a fork.

9.   Stir in the capers and parsley. Serve immediately. Enjoy!

Chicken, Peppers and Red Onion kabobs
Servings: 6

Ingredients

- 3 large garlic cloves, crushed

- 3 tbsp. finely chopped fresh rosemary leaves

- 1 1/2 tbsp. finely chopped fresh oregano

- 2 tsp. kosher salt, to taste

- 1/2 tsp. freshly ground black pepper

- 6 tbsp. olive oil

- 1/4 cup fresh lemon juice

- 1 1/2 lb. boneless, skinless chicken breasts, cut into 1 inch pieces

- 1 red bell pepper, cut into 1 inch pieces

- 1 red onion, cut into 1 inch wedges

Directions

1.	In a large bowl, combine garlic, rosemary, oregano, 1 tsp. salt, pepper, 5 tbsp. oil and 3 tbsp. juice.

2.	Add chicken, tossing to coat in marinade.

3.	Cover and refrigerate 30 minutes or up to an hour.

4.	Meanwhile soak wooden skewer in water for about 30 minutes.

5.	Preheat oven to 425°F.

6.	In a small bowl, combine remaining lemon juice, oil and salt.

7.	Thread chicken, peppers and onions onto skewers, alternating as desired. Discard marinade.

8.	Arrange skewers on a foil-lined baking sheet with a rack. Baste skewer with lemon mixture.

9.	Bake, turning occasionally and basting with lemon mixture, 12 minutes or until chicken is no longer pink in the middle and vegetables are tender.

10.	Discard remaining lemon mixture. Serve and enjoy!

Mediterranean Chicken and Orzo
Servings: 4

Ingredients:

- 1 cup low sodium chicken broth

- 1 medium onion, halved and sliced

- 1 pound boneless, skinless chicken breasts, trimmed

- 2 medium tomatoes, chopped

- 1 lemon, zested and juiced
- 1/2 tsp. salt
- 3/4 cup whole wheat orzo
- 2 tbsp. fresh parsley, chopped
- 1 tsp. herbs de Provence
- 1/2 tsp. black pepper
- 1/3 cup black olives, quartered

Directions

1. Put chicken, tomatoes, onion, lemon zest, juice, broth, salt, black pepper and herbs de Provence in a slow cooker.

2. Cover the lid and cook on High for about 2 hours.

3. Mix well and add orzo and olives to the dish.

4. Allow it to cook for about 30 more minutes more on High.

5. Garnish with parsley and serve warm. Enjoy!

Chicken with Tomato Sauce
Servings: 4

Ingredients

- 1/2 tsp. salt, divided

- 2 (8 oz.) chicken breasts, boneless and skinless, sliced into 4 equal sized pieces

- 1/2 tsp. black pepper, divided

- 3 tbsp. olive oil, divided
- 2 tbsp. shallots, sliced
- 1/4 cup balsamic vinegar
- 1 tbsp. garlic, minced
- 1 tbsp. butter
- 1/4 cup white whole wheat flour
- 1/2 cup cherry tomatoes, halved
- 1 cup low-sodium chicken broth
- 1 tbsp. fennel seeds, toasted and lightly crushed

Directions

1. Season the chicken pieces with salt and black pepper.

2. Spread flour in a dish and dredge the chicken through it.

3. Shake off the excess flour and keep aside.

4. Heat 2 tablespoons of cooking oil in a large skillet and add 2 pieces of chicken at a time.

5. Sear for about 3 minutes on each side and transfer this chicken to a plate.

6. Cover with a foil and heat the remaining oil in the same pan.

7. Add tomatoes and shallots and cook for about 2 minutes until soft.

8. Pour in the vinegar and cook for about 45 seconds.

9. Add broth, garlic, fennel seeds, salt and black pepper and cook for about 5 minutes.

10. Stir in the butter and serve warm. Enjoy!

Lemon-Thyme Chicken
Servings: 4

Ingredients

- 1 tsp. crushed dried thyme, divided

- 1/4 tsp. black pepper

- 4 small skinless, boneless chicken breast halves

- 1 lemon thinly sliced

- 4 tsp. extra-virgin olive oil, divided

- 1/2 tsp. salt

- 1 pound fingerling potatoes halved lengthwise

- 2 garlic cloves, minced

Directions

1. Heat 2 teaspoons of oil in a skillet over medium heat and add ½ teaspoon thyme, potatoes, salt, and black pepper.

2. Cook for about 1 minute and cook, covered for about 12 minutes, stirring occasionally.

3. Push the potatoes to a side and add rest of the oil and chicken.

4. Sear the chicken pieces for 5 minutes on each side and sprinkle with thyme.

5. Arrange lemon slices over the chicken and cover the pan again.

6. Cook for about 10 minutes and dish out to serve warm. Enjoy!

Spiced Chicken, Chickpeas and Peppers
Servings: 4

Ingredients

- 1 tbsp. olive oil

- 1 onion, chopped

- 4 garlic cloves, minced
- 2 lb. chicken thighs, boneless, fat-trimmed and sliced into medium- sized chunks
- 1 cup tomato sauce
- 2 tomatoes, cut into medium-sized chunks
- 2 red peppers, sliced in half
- 1/2 tsp. red pepper flakes
- 1 can chickpeas
- 1 tsp. cumin
- 1 tsp. dried parsley
- 1/2 tsp. coriander
- 1 tsp. salt
- 1/2 tsp. black pepper

Directions

1. Add the olive oil to the oven.
2. Sauté the onions and garlic for 5 minutes.
3. Add the chicken cubes.
4. Cook for 5 minutes.
5. Add the rest of the ingredients.
6. Seal the skillet. Turn to manual.
7. Cook on low for 10 minutes.
8. Release the pressure naturally.
9. Serve with pita bread or salad. Enjoy!

Lemon Garlic Chicken
Servings: 4

Ingredients

- 1 tbsp. avocado oil
- 1 onion, diced
- 2 lb. chicken breasts
- 5 garlic cloves, minced
- 1 tsp. salt
- 1 tsp. dried parsley
- 1/2 cup chicken broth
- 1/4 cup white cooking wine
- 1/4 tsp. paprika
- 1 tbsp. lemon juice
- 3 tsp. arrowroot flour

Directions

1. Pre heat the oven and add the avocado oil.
2. Put the onions inside the oven.
3. Cook for 5 minutes.
4. Add the rest of the ingredients, except for the flour.
5. Cover the skillet. Choose the poultry setting.
6. Release the pressure naturally.
7. Take ¼ cup of the cooking liquid from the skillet.

8. Add the arrowroot flour to this liquid.

9. Pour it back into the skillet. Stir well.

10. Serve while warm. Enjoy!

Shredded Chicken with Marinara

Servings: 4

Ingredients

- 4 lb. chicken breast
- 1/2 cup chicken broth
- 1 tsp. salt
- 1/2 tsp. black pepper
- 2 cups marinara sauce

Directions

1. Put all the ingredients except the marinara sauce in your oven.

2. Seal the skillet. Set the skillet to manual.

3. Cook on high for 20 minutes.

4. Release the pressure quickly.

5. Shred the chicken.

6. Set the skillet to the sauté function.

7. Add the marinara sauce.

8. Simmer for 5 minutes.

9. Serve with rice or green salad. Enjoy!

Garlic Herbed Chicken Breasts

Servings: 4

Ingredients

- 3 tbsp. olive oil

- 3 tbsp. lemon juice

- 3 garlic cloves, crushed and minced

- 3 tbsp. fresh parsley, chopped

- 1/2 tsp. dried oregano

- 1 tsp. paprika

- 1/2 tsp. salt

- 1/2 tsp. pepper

- 4 chicken breasts, boneless and skinless

Directions

1. In a bowl, mix the olive oil, lemon juice, garlic, parsley, oregano and paprika.

2. Sprinkle the salt and pepper onto the chicken.

3. Marinate in the spice mixture for 30 minutes in the refrigerator.

4. Brown the chicken for 10 minutes.

5. Serve with pasta or salad. Enjoy!

Chicken with Red Pepper Sauce

Servings: 4

Ingredients

- 1/2 tsp. salt

- 1/4 tsp. black pepper

- 1/4 cup red peppers, chopped

- 4 tbsp. olive oil, divided

- 2 tsp. Italian seasoning, divided

- 3 tsp. garlic, minced

- 4 chicken breasts, skinless and boneless

- 1 cup heavy cream

- 2 tbsp. feta cheese, crumbled

- 1/4 cup fresh basil, chopped

Directions

1. Mix together the salt, pepper, red peppers, half of the olive oil, the Italian seasoning and garlic.

2. Put the mixture in a food processor.

3. Pulse until smooth.

4. Pour the remaining oil into the oven.

5. Brown the chicken for 10 minutes.

6. Stir in the red pepper mixture.

7. Seal the skillet. Turn to the manual setting.

8. Cook on high for 10 minutes.

9. Release the pressure quickly.

10. Press the sauté mode.

11. Stir in the heavy cream.

12. Simmer for 5 minutes.

13. Serve with the feta cheese and basil. Enjoy!

Creamy Chicken

Servings: 4

Ingredients

- 1 1/2 lb. chicken breasts
- Salt and pepper, to taste
- 2 tbsp. oil
- 1 tsp. garlic, minced
- 14 oz. canned marinated artichoke hearts, drained
- 1/4 cup sun-dried tomatoes, julienned
- 1/3 cup kalamata olives, pitted
- 1 1/4 cups half and half cream
- 1/4 cup parmesan cheese
- 2 tbsp. fresh basil, sliced
- 1/4 cup feta cheese

Directions

1. Season the chicken breasts with the salt and pepper.
2. Pour the oil into the oven.
3. Cook the chicken until brown.
4. Remove the chicken and transfer to a plate.
5. Add the garlic and sauté for 30 seconds.
6. Add the olives, artichokes, tomatoes, olives and cream.
7. Put the chicken back into the oven.
8. Simmer until the sauce has thickened.
9. Add the Parmesan cheese.
10. Serve with the basil and feta cheese. Enjoy!

Olive Chicken

Servings: 4

Ingredients

- 1 tbsp. lime juice
- 1/4 cup olive oil
- 1/4 tsp. dried oregano
- 1/2 cup ripe green olives
- 1/2 tbsp. garlic, crushed
- 1/4 tsp. lime zest
- 1 tsp. honey
- 1/4 tsp. red pepper flakes
- Salt and pepper, to taste
- 2 lb. chicken

- 1/4 cup dry white wine

- 1 tsp. cornstarch

Directions

1. In a bowl, combine the lime juice, olive oil, oregano, olives, garlic, lime zest, honey, red pepper flakes, salt and pepper.

2. Marinate the chicken in this mixture in the refrigerator for 2 hours.

3. Put the chicken inside the oven.

4. Seal the oven. Select the poultry setting.

5. Release the pressure naturally.

6. Uncover the oven. Stir in the cornstarch mixed with white wine.

7. Press the sauté function.

8. Simmer for 10 minutes. Serve and enjoy!

Baked Lemon Chicken

Servings: 4

Ingredients

- 1/2 cup olive oil
- 3 garlic cloves, minced
- 1/4 cup lemon juice
- 1/2 tsp. salt
- 1/4 tsp. pepper
- 1/2 tsp. dried thyme
- 1/8 tsp. ground nutmeg
- 1/8 tsp. ground allspice
- 4 chicken breasts, boneless and skinless
- 1 lemon, sliced
- 1/4 cup chicken stock
- For the Spice Blend:
- 1 tsp. paprika
- 1/4 tsp. garlic salt
- 1/4 tsp. lemon pepper seasoning
- 1/8 tsp. ground allspice

Directions

1.   In a bowl, combine the oil, garlic, lemon juice, salt, pepper, thyme, nutmeg and allspice.

2.   Marinate the chicken in this mixture in the refrigerator for 1 hour.

3.   Pour in the chicken stock.

4.   Place the chicken inside the oven.

5.   Top with the lemon slices.

6.   In another bowl, mix the ingredients in the spice blend.

7.   Sprinkle the spice blend on top of the chicken and lemon slices.

8.   Seal the skillet. Cook on low for 30 minutes. Serve and enjoy!

Lemon Chicken with Greek Olives

Servings: 4

Ingredients

- Salt and pepper, to taste

- 8 chicken thighs

- 3 tbsp. olive oil
- 12 garlic cloves, crushed
- 4 cups yellow onion, chopped
- 4 tbsp. fresh oregano leaves, divided
- 1/2 cup black olives
- 1/2 cup green olives
- 1 tbsp. lemon juice

Directions

1. Rub the salt and pepper onto the chicken thighs.
2. Add the olive oil to the oven.
3. Cook the chicken for 5 minutes.
4. Add the garlic cloves and cook for 1 minute.
5. Add the onions, oregano, black olives, and green olives.
6. Cook for 2 minutes, stirring frequently.
7. Drizzle with the lemon juice before serving. Enjoy!

Chicken Orzo

Servings: 4

Ingredients

- 6 chicken thighs, skinless
- 1 tsp. salt
- 1 1/2 tsp. paprika
- 1/2 tsp. ground turmeric

- 1 1/2 tsp. ground allspice
- 1 tbsp. olive oil
- 1 onion, diced
- 6 garlic cloves
- 4 mushrooms, sliced
- 1 stick celery, diced
- 1 carrot, diced
- 2 cups cherry tomatoes
- 1 tbsp. lemon juice
- 8 oz. orzo noodles, cooked
- 1/2 cup parsley

Directions

1.   Season the chicken thighs with salt, paprika, turmeric and allspice.

2.   Allow to sit in the refrigerator for 10 minutes.

3.   Coat the oven with the olive oil.

4.   Brown the chicken for 5 minutes.

5.   Put the chicken on a platter.

6.   Add the onions, garlic, mushrooms, celery and carrots into the skillet.

7.   Cook for 10 minutes, stirring occasionally.

8.   Add the chicken stock, tomatoes and lemon juice. Mix well.

9.   Put the chicken back into the skillet.

10.   Place the lid on the skillet and seal. Turn it to manual.

11.   Cook on high for 10 minutes.

12.   Release the pressure quickly.

13.   Stir in the cooked orzo.

14.   Simmer for 1 minute.

15.   Garnish with parsley before serving. Enjoy!

Chicken Shawarma

Servings: 4

- 1/2 tsp. turmeric
- 1 tsp. paprika

- 1/4 tsp. garlic salt

- 1 tsp. ground cumin

- 1/4 tsp. ground allspice

- 1/4 tsp. chili powder

- 1/8 tsp. ground cinnamon

- Salt and pepper, to taste

- 1 lb. chicken breast, boneless, skinless, sliced into strips

- 1 lb. chicken thighs, boneless and skinless, sliced into strips

- 1 cup chicken stock

- Green salad, for serving

Directions

1.   Combine the turmeric, paprika, garlic salt, cumin, allspice, chili powder, ground cinnamon, salt and pepper in a bowl.

2.   Coat the chicken cubes with this spice mixture.

3.   Marinate for 30 minutes.

4.   Add the chicken stock .

5.   Add the chicken with the spice mixture. Mix well.

6.   Seal the skillet. Set it to the poultry mode.

7.   Cook for 15 minutes.

8.   Release the pressure naturally.

9.   Serve with the green salad. Enjoy!

Chicken Tikka Masala

Servings: 4

Ingredients

- 2 tbsp. olive oil

- 1 onion, chopped
- 1 inch ginger, chopped
- 3 garlic cloves, crushed and minced
- 1 tsp. garam masala
- 2 tsp. paprika
- 2 tsp. cumin

- 1 tsp. ground turmeric
- 1/4 tsp. cayenne pepper
- 1 tsp. ground coriander
- 14 oz. canned diced tomatoes with juice
- 1 1/2 lb. chicken breast, boneless and skinless
- 1/2 cup chicken broth
- 1/2 cup canned coconut milk
- 1 tbsp. arrowroot starch
- 1 tbsp. lemon juice
- 1 cup fresh basil, chopped

Directions

1. Pre heat the oven
2. Add the olive oil.
3. Cook the onions, ginger and garlic for 3 minutes.
4. Add all the spices.
5. Pour in the tomatoes.
6. Place the chicken on top.

7. Pour in the broth.

8. Seal the skillet. Select the manual mode.

9. Cook on high for 7 minutes.

10. Release the pressure quickly.

11. Take the chicken out of the skillet.

12. Shred the meat.

13. Place the shredded chicken inside the skillet. Set the skillet to Sauté.

14. Pour in the coconut milk, arrowroot starch and lemon juice.

15. Simmer for 5 minutes.

16. Garnish with fresh basil before serving. Enjoy!

Hasselback Caprese Chicken

Servings: 4

Ingredients

- 1/2 tsp. salt, divided

- 3 oz. fresh mozzarella, halved and sliced
- 2 chicken breasts, boneless and skinless
- 1/2 tsp. black pepper, divided
- 1 medium tomato, sliced
- 1/4 cup prepared pesto
- 2 tbsp. extra virgin olive oil
- 8 cups broccoli florets

Directions

1.   Preheat the oven to 370 degrees F and grease a baking sheet.

2.   Season the chicken with salt and black pepper.

3.   Insert mozzarella and tomato slices in the chicken cuts.

4.   Brush with pesto and transfer the chicken breasts on the baking sheet.

5.   Toss broccoli with oil, salt and black pepper in a large bowl.

6.   Spread the broccoli mixture around the chicken and bake for about 25 minutes.

7.   Dish out and serve warm. Enjoy!

Olive Chicken

Servings: 6

Ingredients

- 2 tbsp. white wine
- 3 garlic cloves, minced
- 2 tsp. olive oil
- 6 chicken breast halves, skinless and boneless
- 1/2 cup onions, diced
- 1/2 cup white wine
- 1 tbsp. fresh basil, chopped
- 2 fennel bulbs, sliced in half
- Salt and black pepper, to taste
- 3 cups tomatoes, chopped
- 2 tsp. fresh thyme, chopped
- 1/2 cup kalamata olives
- 1/4 cup fresh parsley, chopped

Directions

1. Heat oil with 2 tablespoons white wine in a large skillet on medium heat.

2. Add chicken and cook for about 6 minutes per side.

3. Transfer the chicken to a plate and stir in garlic.

4. Sauté for about 30 seconds and add onions.

5.   Sauté for about 3 minutes and stir in fennel and tomatoes.

6.   Allow it to boil and lower the heat.

7.   Add half cup white wine and cook for about 10 minutes.

8.   Stir in basil and thyme and cook for about 5 minutes.

9.   Return the cooked chicken to the skillet.

10.   Cover the cooking pan and cook on low heat.

11.   Stir in parsley and olives and cook for about 1 minute.

12.   Adjust seasoning with salt and black pepper.

Serve and enjoy!